Contents

Some words are shown in bold, **like this**. You can find out what they mean by looking in the glossary.

Writing David's story

Anne Holm, the author of *I am David*, was born on 10 September, 1922, in a town called Aal in Denmark. She trained as a journalist then moved on to working in television and writing for teenage magazines. She later began writing novels for young adults.

A story of hope

Titled simply *David* in the Danish edition, Anne Holm wrote her novel because she thought that children needed "real" and "valuable" literature. As David himself says in the story, "Children have a right to know everything that's true". The story Holm wrote is about finding the truth.

Anne Holm wanted to create an exciting page-turner for young readers that would tackle important subjects such as warfare, refugees, and the responsibilities of freedom. Her main character, David, is a clever twelve-year-old boy trapped in unimaginable circumstances.

David has lived in a **prison camp** in Eastern Europe for most of his life. In the former **Soviet Union** children went to camps if their parents were sent. Once in the camp, children and even babies were separated from their parents and lived in appalling conditions. Few of the children survived. David knows nothing about his own parents, where he comes from, or why he is in the camp. He does not even know what he looks like. All he knows is his name and age. One day, without any explanation, a guard arranges for David to escape. He leaves the camp with only a few items. Sensing that the other guards are hot on his heels, David fears his wonderful new freedom will only last a few "moments".

The writer of *I am David* is Anne Holm, pictured. She died in 1998.

THE STORY BEHIND...

www.heinemann.co.uk/library
Visit our website to find out more information about Heinemann Library books.

To order:
☎ Phone 44 (0) 1865 888066
🗎 Send a fax to 44 (0) 1865 314091
🖥 Visit the Heinemann Bookshop at www.heinemann.co.uk/library to browse our catalogue and order online.

First published in Great Britain by
Heinemann Library, Halley Court, Jordan Hill,
Oxford, OX2 8EJ, part of Harcourt Education.
Heinemann is a registered trademark of
Harcourt Education Ltd.

© Harcourt Education Ltd 2007
First published in paperback in 2008
The moral right of the proprietor has
been asserted.

Editorial: Louise Galpine, Lucy Beevor,
    and Rosie Gordon
Design: Richard Parker and
    Tinstar Design
Picture Research: Melissa Allison and
    Ginny Stroud–Lewis
Production: Vicki Fitzgerald

Originated by Modern Age
Printed and bound in China by Leo Paper Group

13 digit ISBN 978 0 431 08169 4 (hardback)
11 10 09 08 07
10 9 8 7 6 5 4 3 2 1

13 digit ISBN 978 0 431 08183 0 (paperback)
12 11 10 09 08
10 9 8 7 6 5 4 3 2 1

British Library Cataloguing in Publication Data
Colson, Mary
The story behind Anne Holm's I am David. –
(History in literature)
839.8'1374
A full catalogue record for this book is
available from the British Library.

Acknowledgements
The publishers would like to thank the following
for permission to reproduce photographs/quotes:
Alamy Images pp. 16 (J Marshall – Tribaleye
Images), 18 (Popperfoto); Corbis p. 42, pp.
49 (Benjamin Lowy), 36 (Bettman), 25 (Ira
Nowinski), 46 (Reuters/ Fabrizio Bensch), 41
(Thorne Anderson); David King Collection pp. 13,
17, 32; Empics p. 44 (AP); Getty Images pp. 21,
26, 33, 37 (Hulton Archive), 35 (Hulton Archive/
American Stock), 47 (Photonica/Deborah Raven),
9, 28 (Time Life Pictures); Rex Features p. 43
(Christopher Fitzgerald), 6, 8 (Roger Viollet), 20
(SIPA); RIA-Novosti pp. 12, 14, 30, 31, 38, 39;
Robert Harding p. 5 (Ken Gillham); Scanpix
Denmark p. 4; The Kobal Collection pp. 40
(Goskino), 19 (Melampo, Cinematografica/Strizzi,
Sergio); Topfoto pp. 15, 45, pp. 29 (AP), 27
(RIA Novosti), 34 (UPPA).

1)   Basic text
1a) From I am David by Anne Holm, with
permission of Egmont UK Ltd, London – UK rights
1b) Reproduced from North to Freedom later
published as I am David by Anne Holm with
permission of Harcourt Inc – USA and Canada
rights
2)   Page 11 – Reproduced with permission
of Curtis Brown on behalf of The Estate of
Winston Churchill

Cover photograph of Anne Holm reproduced with
permission of Scanpix Denmark. Background
photographs reproduced with permission of
Photos.com.

The publishers would like to thank Professor
Martyn Rady for his assistance in the preparation
of this book.

Two opposing systems

Although Holm never gives a precise date for her story, the novel features cars, electricity, and the Queen of England. This leads us to believe that it must be after Elizabeth II became Queen of England in 1952.

At that time, the developed world was divided between two opposing political systems, **democracy** and **communism**.

What we now know as the **Cold War** had broken out between the United States and the Soviet Union (USSR) as each strove to become the dominant world power.

Holm's aim in the novel is to show the evils of political systems that do not allow people to speak, or even think, their own thoughts.

Anne Holm was born in Aal, Denmark, in 1922.

A climate of fear

In order to understand how David could have been brought up in a camp, it is important to look at the world situation in the first half of the 20th century. Anne Holm was writing her novel in the early 1960s, at the height of the Cold War. These were times of **persecution** and extreme political ideas and beliefs.

David and his parents lived in a country where the political situation was "dangerous" and where his father "wasn't careful". We are never told the name of the country that David was imprisoned in, but it is likely that Anne Holm was describing Bulgaria. Bulgaria is due north of Salonica, and David was told to escape south from his prison camp to Salonica.

In 1952, Bulgaria was ruled by **communists** and was largely cut off from the Western world. The country was under the political influence of the Soviet Union and its leader Joseph Stalin. Meaning "man of steel", Stalin was a ruthless **dictator** who governed through fear and force, imprisoning anyone whom he considered an opponent or threat. In both the USSR and Bulgaria, secret police forces (whom David calls "they") enforced state security. Intimidation, violence, and executions were some of their methods of control. Anyone who publicly disagreed with the system was sentenced to hard labour and sent to camps called the **Gulag**.

Labour camps existed all around the Soviet Union and other communist countries. Inmates were put to work in all weathers, digging railways and canals, logging, mining, and working in factories and on farms. Here, inmates are seen building a factory in Siberia in 1931.

Life in the camp

The Gulag was a system of forced labour or "re-education". Millions of people were imprisoned in the camps, which were created during the 1920s and reached their peak after World War II, the period in which *I am David* is set. It is estimated that under Stalin there were over 450 camps in the USSR alone, with a steady prison population of around 2 million people. There were sometimes even special camps for children, for disabled people, and for mothers with babies.

In his camp, David has watched people starve and seen guards who "did not leave off striking till their victims fainted". Cruel treatment and back-breaking work are everyday events. He has learnt to survive by not thinking further than his next meal. Everything that David knows has been told to him by his only friend, Johannes, who is now dead.

In 1952, the International League for the Rights of Man documented the existence of more than 400 forced labour camps in Central and Eastern Europe with around 100 in Bulgaria alone. Some of these camps were still in use as late as the 1970s.

A SYMBOL OF FREEDOM

Anne Holm never identifies the camp's location or the nationality of the guards. Her aim is to show that extreme political systems do not work. Freedoms of speech and thought are basic human rights that should apply wherever the location.

WORK IN THE CAMP

Prisoners were forced to work as builders, miners, or in whatever jobs the communist plans for national development required. The camps produced much of the Soviet Union's coal and timber, as well as other valuable resources. Lack of suitable clothing, small amounts of food, and the bitter cold of winter meant death rates were high.

SECRET WORSHIP

*During the 1920s and 1930s in the USSR, over 50,000 priests along with hundreds of nuns, rabbis, and other religious leaders were executed, **exiled**, or sent to labour camps. In remote parts some priests survived and continued to worship. There are even stories of prisoners in camps who managed to celebrate religious festivals such as Christmas.*

Religion was banned under communism. Stalin ordered the destruction of many holy places, such as this church tower in Iaroslav, Soviet Union. By the beginning of World War II, nearly 5,000 synagogues had been closed and only 500 churches out of 54,000 remained open.

Freedom to believe

I am David was written at a time when human rights were at the centre of international political debate. **Nazi** Germany's persecution of the Jews in World War II had been revealed to a shocked world only two decades before, and reports of Soviet labour camps were gradually seeping into Western newspapers. Through David's story, therefore, Anne Holm drew on both Nazi and communist systems of persecution to highlight the brutality of extreme political systems.

In 1948, the newly created **United Nations** published a document designed to prevent further **violations** of human rights. The "Universal Declaration of Human Rights" is a list of rights for all people. It states that no one shall be subjected to cruel treatment or punishment. David has no rights. He has been denied the human right outlined in Article 18 of the declaration, which states that everyone has the right to freedom of thought and religion.

The state religion

The state "religion" of the Communist regime was atheism, a disbelief in the existence of God. Under Stalin, churches, mosques, and synagogues, along with religious schools and monasteries, were closed. The publication of religious materials was banned and religious leaders were executed or – like the Italian priest in David's camp – sent to prison camps. On his journey, David is instinctively drawn towards churches, and is also struck by the beauty of nature. David eventually chooses his own God. This is the first major freedom or human right that David embraces after his escape. As a Christian herself, Anne Holm defines David's God in Christian terms. David refers to the god of "green pastures" and "still waters", both phrases taken from the Bible.

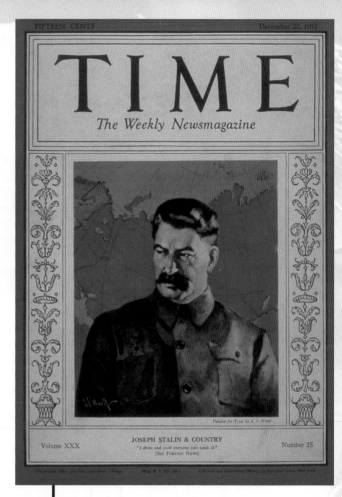

Stalin's political influence was so great that some sectors of the **capitalist** West respected certain aspects of his leadership, particularly during World War II. The US magazine *Time* voted Stalin "Man of the Year" in both 1939 and 1943.

Moral guidance

In the camp, David is guided by his friend Johannes who teaches him right from wrong and protects him from the worst of life in the "wicked place". David is devastated by Johannes' death, but later finds that Johannes' spirit is a comfort to him on the first part of his journey. This is David's first religious experience.

David's God gradually takes the place of Johannes as David's source of comfort. David goes through an emotional and spiritual change. He starts believing that he might remain free and decides he wants to live. At first David knows "nothing about what people ought to do for their God", but his prayers throughout the novel show his increasing understanding of the nature of faith.

An epic journey

Before his escape, the camp's fence is the limit of David's world and knowledge. His route to Denmark is not only a physical journey, but also one of hope and self-discovery. This is how David's strange new world looked in the 1950s.

The map shows the course David's journey takes and the experiences he goes through along the way. In the early 1950s, Europe was divided according to political ideas. The **Warsaw Pact** countries were allies of Russia and were governed by communist governments, while the **North Atlantic Treaty Organization (NATO)** consisted of the democracies of the West including the United States, the United Kingdom, and France.

Key to map

1. Bulgaria had one of the strictest Soviet-loyal governments of Eastern Europe. Freedom of speech and travel were not allowed. Here in the camp, David lives anonymously behind fences, guarded by guns and dogs.

2. In 1952, Italy was a young democracy after the fall of the dictator Mussolini at the end of World War II. Here, David meets the del 'Varchi family, with whom he stays for a time, learns to smile, and chooses a god.

3. Switzerland was **neutral** during World War II and remained so afterwards. Here, David learns about his family through a chance encounter with a Danish artist. He later suffers terrible cruelty at the hands of a farmer.

4. After World War II, Germany was divided into two countries, East Germany and West Germany. East Germany was a communist state, while West Germany was democratic. By 1961, the capital of East Germany, Berlin, was divided between the two countries. Families were divided by barriers, soldiers, and watchtowers. It is in Germany that David has to overcome a final confrontation with "them" before he can go on to Denmark.

5. The Nazis **occupied** Denmark during World War II. At the end of the war, the **monarchy** and democratic government were restored. In Denmark, David finds his mother and a country where he can "live in safety".

In 1946, Winston Churchill summarized the political situation saying,

From Stettin in the Baltic to Trieste in the Adriatic an iron curtain has descended across the Continent.

Liberating occupied Eastern Europe from Nazi Germany had led to occupation by Stalin's Soviet Union.

A CONFLICT OF IDEAS

*The end of World War II saw an estimated 15 million people displaced. People like David looked for new lives in North America or Western Europe as they rushed to escape the newly installed communist **regimes**.*

*After World War II, the democracies of the West such as the United Kingdom and the United States, were concerned about Soviet aggression and the spread of communism. They established the North Atlantic Treaty Organization (NATO) in 1949. A collective defence agreement was made: if one member state is attacked it is considered an attack on all. In response, the Soviet Union and its communist **allies** created their own **bloc**, or group of countries, that agreed to defend each other against Western hostility. In 1955, this agreement, called the Warsaw Pact, was signed.*

Victims of politics

Anne Holm created David's story against the tense political backdrop of East and West, secrecy versus openness. In order to understand how she used history both as inspiration and for moral force it is necessary to look at the details of communism, and the causes of the Cold War.

A political theory

The German philosopher Karl Marx wrote the founding document of communism *The Communist **Manifesto***, which was published in 1848. Marx, and his co-writer Friedrich Engels, believed that it was the workers of society who held ultimate power, and that a **revolution** by the workers would create a more equal society. This theory divided society into classes, the workers, the middle class (or **bourgeoisie**), and the upper class (or **aristocracy**). The upper classes were considered "class enemies" because they **exploited** the workers. Once communists had seized power in Russia and after 1945 in Eastern Europe, "class enemies" were either sent to the Gulag or shot. In a communist society the people as a whole – not individuals – own factories, businesses, land, and industry. Karl Marx famously said, "Philosophers have only interpreted the world, in various ways; the point, however, is to change it." For millions of people living in the Eastern bloc under an extreme version of communism, Marx's theory would indeed change their world.

Vladimir Ilich Lenin (1870–1924)

Before the Russian Revolution, Lenin had been arrested a number of times and even exiled in Siberia for five years. He believed passionately in the rights of working people, but did not live to see where his "Workers' Revolution" would ultimately lead. An assassination attempt in 1918 left bullets lodged in his neck and one of his lungs. This led to Lenin suffering four strokes, the last of which killed him in 1924. This painting known as Lenin Declares Soviet Power *is by Vladimir Serov, from 1947.*

Centuries of exploitation

Tsars ruled Russia until 1917. For centuries, the tsars and the class of noble landowners exploited the large peasant population working on the land. Under a system called **serfdom** peasants were bought and sold with the land as if they were possessions. During World War I, demand for the production of war supplies meant that more factory workers were needed. Peasants moved out of the country and into towns and cities hoping to find work. The cities soon became overpopulated and living conditions grew rapidly worse. As more food was needed for the soldiers fighting in World War I, supplies in the cities grew scarce. By 1917, mass hunger threatened many of the larger cities and riots broke out.

A year of turmoil

Following the riots, the Russian Revolution took place in two phases in 1917, one in February, and one in October. Tsar Nicholas II was **deposed** and the communist **Bolshevik** Party, led by Vladimir Lenin, seized power. Lenin had already caught the public imagination with various pamphlets. In these pamphlets he presented a great future for ordinary Russians and told them it was within their reach. After the Revolution, Lenin and his party established the world's first communist state.

The head of a monument to Tsar Alexander III lies destroyed during the Russian Revolution, Moscow, 1917.

After the Revolution, the tsar and his family were held prisoner in Siberia before being executed. Some historians believe the tsar's family, the Romanovs, were smuggled out of the country. However, recent DNA tests on uncovered human remains prove the family died in 1918.

CHANGING STATES

*The Union of Soviet **Socialist** Republics (USSR), or Soviet Union, was formed in 1922. The Soviet government was a model for future communist nations such as Bulgaria. It was run by the only permitted political party, the Communist Party of the Soviet Union. This union of fifteen republics lasted until 1991. After this a smaller union of republics, including Russia, was called the Confederation of Independent States (CIS).*

Civil war

After the Revolution, a civil war broke out in Russia between the "Reds", who were the communists, and the "Whites", who believed in more gradual change. The war led to the suffering and death of millions of people. Lenin and the Reds imprisoned thousands of "class-enemies" and "counter-revolutionaries", aristocrats or wealthy people who were persecuted, not for what they had done but for who they were. The Revolution had been inspired by a desire to create a fairer society by deposing the **corrupt** tsars. In reality, the regime that replaced the tsars turned out to be even worse.

Power struggle

In the early 1920s, Stalin was becoming an important power within the Communist Party. This concerned Lenin who wrote a document before he died proposing changes to the power structure of the Party. Known as "Lenin's Testament", it warned against Stalin's increasing "authority", but Stalin's friends kept the document hidden.

Following Lenin's death, Stalin outmanoeuvred his main rival Leon Trotsky and took control of the Communist Party. Trotsky was exiled, but remained politically active abroad. A Stalinist agent, Ramón Mercader, assassinated Trotsky in Mexico in 1940 by driving an ice pick into his skull.

THE POWER AND POLITICS OF WRITING

Anne Holm wrote her story in a democratic country where writers were free from political interference. This was not the case in the USSR. Lenin believed that literature and art could be exploited for political, as well as educational purposes. As a result, the Party quickly took control of newspapers, book publishing, bookshops, and libraries.

*Elsewhere in the world, writers were trying to bring attention to the dangerous political situation in the USSR. George Orwell's novel Animal Farm is a **satire** of the Russian Revolution and life under Stalin. In Orwell's story, the animals of Manor Farm revolt against the oppressive Farmer Jones in order to run the farm themselves on **egalitarian** principles. The pig leaders Napoleon (Stalin) and Snowball (Trotsky) become corrupted by power and a new **tyranny** is established. Snowball is driven out, and ambitious Napoleon is left in charge. Animal Farm ends up being run according to a list of commandments, the most famous being, "All animals are equal, but some are more equal than others."*

Icons from a destroyed church in the Soviet Union are placed on to a truck to be burned. Stalin (and later Hitler in Nazi Germany) ordered the destruction of art and books created by people thought to be "class enemies", such as Albert Einstein. People were sent to prison camps for even translating banned books.

The hammer and sickle were the symbols of the communist Soviet Union. The tools represent the workers uniting to build a new egalitarian state.

Building a superpower

By 1922, the Soviet Union was the poorest nation in Europe. World War I had devastated the country and killed millions of people. Stalin had big plans for national economic development, and he also wanted to minimize political opposition.

The Gulag and prisoners like David and Johannes played a key role in building and development projects across the Eastern bloc. Gulag prisoners built whole new towns, railways, and part of the Moscow Metro. Rapid industrialization and **collectivized** farming were the two key aims of Stalin's plans. Within 25 years the USSR was transformed from a poor agricultural nation to a global **superpower**.

A campaign of fear

Stalin wanted to get rid of anyone who might oppose him. His **purges** controlled society through fear, political terror, and **ethnic** persecution. People from all levels of Soviet society, from Communist Party officials to peasants, were shot or arrested by the secret police, the feared NKVD (later known as the KGB). Writers, intellectuals, scientists, artists, and priests were all rounded up along with anyone who was believed to be anti-Stalin. The purges continued until Stalin's death in 1953.

People informed on their neighbours to find favour with the authorities and protect themselves. The sailor who finds David stowed away on the ship to Italy considers turning him in to the captain, but does not because "that was just what those eyes expected him to do". David is "familiar with treachery", and the sailor recognizes this and acts with kindness.

Between 1937 and 1938 alone at least 700,000 people were executed in the Soviet Union. An estimated 1.5 million people of various ethnic groups were **deported** to Central Asian Republics. Millions were sent to the Gulag and put to work on Stalin's huge industrial projects such as railways, canals, buildings, and anywhere that labour was in short supply.

EXILE OR RE-EDUCATION

There were two main methods of punishment for Stalin's political opponents – exile or prison. Exile meant forced relocation to a remote village, while prison meant enclosure behind barriers. Having outlawed religion, Russia had a number of empty, remote monasteries. These were transformed into prisons, such as Solovetsky in the White Sea, which was opened soon after the Revolution. Presented to the world as the new model of punishment, the prisons were supposed to re-educate prisoners through hard work. Prisoners were taught to take pride in working for their country. The work was presented as an honour, and even a glory. If a prisoner failed to meet his daily target, his already pitiful food rations were lessened.

Prisoners emerged from the Gulag once they had served their term and were considered to be pro-Stalin. Official certificates were issued to show they had been pardoned or "rehabilitated".

Gulag inmates toil over the White Sea Canal, 1933. As the guard in the novel tells David, "There's need in a good many places for those strong enough to work."

17

Male and female convicts work together in Taganka Jail, Moscow, around the 1920s. Conditions in prison were often as tough as those in the Gulag.

Child prisoners

Children in the Gulag were separated from their parents and often kept in filthy conditions. They did not help with the labour so were thought of as expensive to keep. Children often died in the camps, and those who survived were usually **malnourished** and **illiterate**. David feels "hate" towards "them", but later discovers that a guard had in fact kept him alive by giving him milk and vitamins twice a week "for as long as David could remember".

Toys and games were unheard of in the camps and children's minds were not stimulated. It is in Italy, with the del 'Varchi family that David realizes that the most important thing the camp has deprived him of is his childhood. He is unable to fully interact with the other children because he does not understand how to play.

A QUESTION OF PERSPECTIVE

The relationship between prisoner and jailer has long captured the imagination of writers. In 1937, French film-maker Jean Renoir directed a film called La Grande Illusion *(The Big Illusion, or Lie). Set in a World War I **prisoner of war (POW)** camp, the story explores the relationship between a German camp **commandant** and a group of French POWs. The story shows that the boundaries between who is good and who is bad are sometimes blurred, as with the character of "the man" in* I am David.*

Escape

Many camps were located within the Arctic Circle where the deadly winter cold made escape impossible. In the novel, David has seen prisoners plan escapes that were never successful because the "chances were too slender". If a guard let a prisoner escape he would be stripped of his uniform and made an inmate himself. David becomes aware that the guard who helped him to escape risked this punishment himself. He says, "If you knew anything about them, then you knew [. . .] the danger the man had risked in letting a prisoner escape. And yet he had done it." At first David is suspicious of the guard's motive, thinking it is a "trap". As he progresses on his journey, however, David begins to think differently about many of his own ideas.

There are numerous stories of imprisoned children with an older, wiser mentor to guide them. Jurek Becker's novel *Jakob the Liar* and Roberto Benigni's film *Life is Beautiful* are both set in **concentration camps** and tell stories of an adult protecting a child from the true horror of where they are. In *I am David*, Johannes is aware of David's lack of knowledge and uses this to protect him. He tells the other prisoners not to "tell the boy anything they might try to worm out of him".

A still from the film *Life is Beautiful,* the story of a father and son imprisoned in a Nazi concentration camp during World War II. The father pretends they are in a game with the Nazis to protect his son from the horrors of the camp.

Efficiency and obedience

Using his vast prison workforce, Stalin was able to put his **Five Year Plans** into action. If he needed more workers, there were more purges. There was a dramatic increase in the number of prisoners during the first Plan in 1928. Improved factory systems meant that the barbed wire and guns needed for the camps could be made quickly. What David calls the "ugly" camps were built in record time.

In his camp, David has seen "only too often what happened if you failed to obey even an ordinary guard". He has witnessed dogs being set on prisoners, and describes it as "one of their pastimes". Punishment in the camps was routine and brutal. Other cruelties included taking prisoners' clothes away and leaving them in their underwear in the bitter winter weather.

The gate of the Vorkuta camp in the Gulag system. The words over the gate say that it is glorious to work hard for the communist state.

One notable Gulag inmate was Aleksandr Solzhenitsyn, a writer arrested for his criticisms of Stalin. He spent eight years in the Gulag followed by permanent exile. In exile, he wrote The Gulag Archipelago, which compared the system of camps to an archipelago, a chain of islands. The book exposed the labour camp system to the outside world using the accounts of hundreds of Gulag survivors. In response, the Soviet authorities deported Solzhenitsyn in 1974 and he settled in the United States. In 1990, his Soviet citizenship was restored. He now lives in Russia where he writes about human rights issues.

A struggle for survival

Many people failed to adapt to the harsh realities of camp life and new prisoner death rates in the Gulag were high, up to 80 percent in some camps. New arrivals at David's camp were, at first, "white and clean all over with no smell about them". David also remembers that after a time in the camp their voices become "flat and grating" as they lost hope of freedom. Even prisoners who had lived in the camps for years did not always survive. In I am David, Johannes simply falls to the ground one day and remains "lying there, dead".

At the age of eighteen, Hungarian writer János Rózsás became a Soviet prisoner of war. He spent nine years in prisons and labour camps. Afterwards he wrote, "In this [. . .] hell of suffering, [. . .] I struggled in the agony caused by starvation, cold and exhausting labour."

It is impossible to give an accurate number for the human losses during Stalin's reign of terror. Thousands died in construction projects alone. It is estimated that if famine and camp death rates are taken into account, Stalin's regime was responsible for between 5 and 10 million deaths.

A world at war

World War II saw the USSR, Germany, and Japan trying to expand their territories. At this time, Anne Holm was studying journalism in Denmark and saw **newsreels** relaying the terrible developments of the war. Her own country was occupied by the Nazis, and all over the world political persecution was escalating.

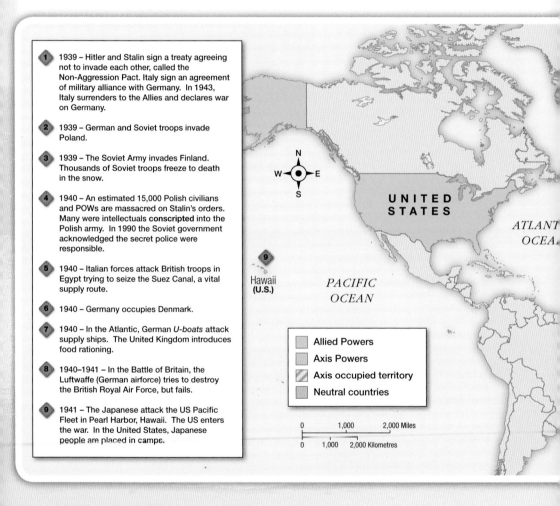

1 1939 – Hitler and Stalin sign a treaty agreeing not to invade each other, called the Non-Aggression Pact. Italy sign an agreement of military alliance with Germany. In 1943, Italy surrenders to the Allies and declares war on Germany.

2 1939 – German and Soviet troops invade Poland.

3 1939 – The Soviet Army invades Finland. Thousands of Soviet troops freeze to death in the snow.

4 1940 – An estimated 15,000 Polish civilians and POWs are massacred on Stalin's orders. Many were intellectuals **conscripted** into the Polish army. In 1990 the Soviet government acknowledged the secret police were responsible.

5 1940 – Italian forces attack British troops in Egypt trying to seize the Suez Canal, a vital supply route.

6 1940 – Germany occupies Denmark.

7 1940 – In the Atlantic, German *U-boats* attack supply ships. The United Kingdom introduces food rationing.

8 1940–1941 – In the Battle of Britain, the Luftwaffe (German airforce) tries to destroy the British Royal Air Force, but fails.

9 1941 – The Japanese attack the US Pacific Fleet in Pearl Harbor, Hawaii. The US enters the war. In the United States, Japanese people are placed in camps.

UNITED STATES

ATLANTIC OCEAN

Hawaii (U.S.)

PACIFIC OCEAN

	Allied Powers
	Axis Powers
	Axis occupied territory
	Neutral countries

0   1,000   2,000 Miles

0   1,000   2,000 Kilometres

The map shows the world as it was during World War II (1939–1945), highlighting some of the major events that occurred during this period. The war engulfed much of the globe and was the largest and deadliest war in history. Germany surrendered to the Allies in May of 1945. The war ended on September 8, 1945 with the surrender of Japan.

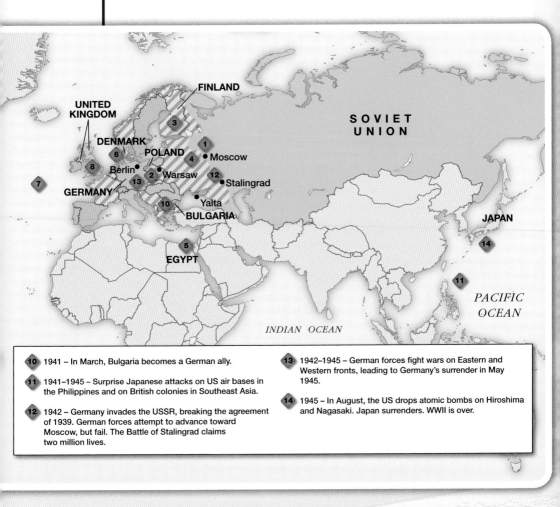

10 1941 – In March, Bulgaria becomes a German ally.

11 1941–1945 – Surprise Japanese attacks on US air bases in the Philippines and on British colonies in Southeast Asia.

12 1942 – Germany invades the USSR, breaking the agreement of 1939. German forces attempt to advance toward Moscow, but fail. The Battle of Stalingrad claims two million lives.

13 1942–1945 – German forces fight wars on Eastern and Western fronts, leading to Germany's surrender in May 1945.

14 1945 – In August, the US drops atomic bombs on Hiroshima and Nagasaki. Japan surrenders. WWII is over.

WORLD WAR II – THE DEATH TOLL

At the end of World War II Stalin said, "The death of one man is a tragedy. The death of millions is a statistic." In some ways, the overwhelming number of deaths meant that the impact of individual tragedies was lost. Worldwide, 50 million people died in World War II.

Racial prejudice

Although Hitler and Stalin's regimes were different, like Stalin, Hitler was a ruler who cruelly abused his authority. In her writing, Anne Holm drew on both Stalin's and Hitler's regimes to show how people like David and his parents became victims of these powerful dictators.

Hitler became Chancellor of Germany in January 1933 and immediately began to wield his power. All soldiers had to swear an oath of **allegiance** to him, while his secret police, the Gestapo, rounded up political opponents and transported them to camps. Like David, the population were soon "familiar with treachery". Stalin and Hitler were both anti-Semitic (anti-Jewish). David is not Jewish, but he knows that "they" imprisoned Jews. Stalin deported thousands of Jews to Central Asia; Hitler had a more deadly plan of **genocide** in mind – a system of **death camps** across Europe.

The system of death camps was connected to train routes. The mass transportation of Jews and other persecuted peoples was then possible from France, Germany, and Hungary. Trains delivered people to the camps from every corner of Hitler's new territory. Many of these camps were located in Poland.

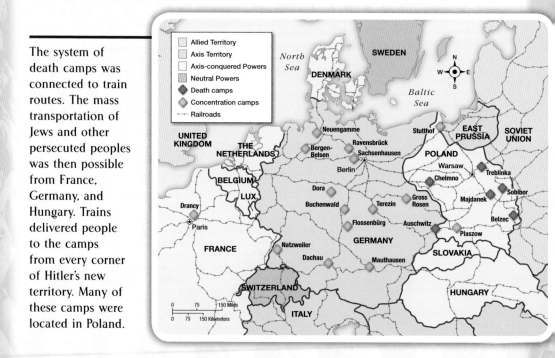

A LIFELINE

The Kindertransport is the name given to the rescue mission that took place nine months prior to the outbreak of World War II, organized by the British Jewish Refugee Committee. Ten thousand unaccompanied children travelled to the United Kingdom from Nazi-occupied countries in sealed trains to escape persecution. The last transport left just two days before war broke out. Upon arrival, some of the children went to foster families or orphanages, and others worked on farms. Most of the children settled in the United Kingdom after the war, but some moved on to Israel or North America. Most of them never saw their parents again.

Life behind walls

Both Hitler and Stalin's prison camps were home to a range of nationalities. The USSR has a variety of languages so in any Gulag population there would have been more than one language spoken. David himself speaks several languages. It was the same in Hitler's camps where Jews were sent from many different countries.

Before Jews were sent to the camps they were contained within ghettos. A ghetto is an area where people from a specific ethnic background or religion live as a group, either through choice or force. In 1939, the Nazis began moving Jews into walled ghettos in Polish cities. Any Jew found leaving was shot. In the Warsaw Ghetto, more than nine people were crammed into each room. With crowded living conditions, little food, and poor sanitation hundreds of thousands of Jews died of disease and starvation. From the ghettos, Jews were transported to concentration camps.

A MIRACULOUS ESCAPE

*During World War II the Jewish population of some European countries was almost wiped out. Danish Jews were luckier. After German occupation, the Danish population organized a rescue operation involving the police, the **resistance**, ordinary people, and fishermen. From a total of around 8,000 people, 7,500 were helped across the sea to neutral Sweden. In the camp, David's faith in humanity and the goodness of people is kept alive through Johannes. "There were some good people – Johannes had told him so."*

In the USSR, under communism, the Gulag presented hard work for the mother country as a noble cause; the Nazi camps used this merely as a cover story. The sign above the entrance to Auschwitz, the largest and deadliest of all the death camps, claimed, *Arbeit macht frei,* or "Work shall make you free." It is estimated that more than a million people were starved, tortured, gassed, and burned at Auschwitz.

Auschwitz survivor Olga Albogen remembers,

> *You know, every wagon, every car was filled with people to capacity. Not a seat for anybody, just standing room, squeezed in. And when they emptied the wagons, thousands and thousands of trains kept on coming from all over Europe [...] It was just unbelievable.*

The death camps

By 1942, Jews and other targeted groups were being transported in trains to various death camps across Nazi-occupied territory. Nazi Germany's systematic killing of European Jews, known as the "Final Solution", had begun. It was genocide on a scale never before seen. Millions were murdered in the gas chambers of death camps such as Auschwitz, Treblinka, and Sobibor.

The SS, Hitler's special police force, were responsible for hiring trains and transporting people to the camps. Trains were commissioned and a one-way group fare was charged. Children under ten years travelled at half-fare and children younger than four years went for free.

Upon arrival at the camp, prisoners were stripped of their belongings, forced to undress, and had their heads shaved to prevent lice infestation. Anyone who was too ill, old, or young to work was sent immediately to the gas chambers. Children were snatched from their parents.

A MUSEUM OF MEMORY

In 1947, Auschwitz became a museum. In 1979, it was awarded World Heritage Site status by the United Nations, and is protected as a site of universal value and education. Auschwitz has become a symbol of human cruelty in the 20th century.

David's eyes have a haunted look. Along his journey, people comment and remark upon his strange look. Survivors from the prison camps often say they recognize other survivors just from the look in their eyes.

Death in the Gulag

In Stalin's Gulag, death was more often the result of harsh conditions. With the help of Johannes and the guard, David is able to survive. By contrast, Hitler's concentration camps were designed specifically as death factories. A prisoner in the Gulag, where the death rate was around 30 percent, had more chance of surviving than someone in a Nazi camp, where the death toll was between 90 and 99 percent. In August 1944, 24,000 people were killed at Auschwitz in a single day.

In the novel, David is suspicious of the guard's motives in helping him to escape. He is convinced it is a trick to shoot him as he escapes and that the guards will find it "amusing". This Russian prisoner of war was shot whilst trying to escape a Nazi prison camp. The guards left his body on view as a warning to others.

TO OBEY IS TO SURVIVE

Being obedient helps David and other inmates survive in the camp. Even after David escapes, he cannot stop obeying the guard and following his instructions. It was sometimes similar for camp guards working in Stalin's and Hitler's regimes. The true story of a young girl named Helga Schneider tells of her mother leaving Helga in 1941 to swear allegiance to Hitler. She became an officer of the SS and worked in the gas chambers in Auschwitz. Asked, after the war, if she was sorry for what she had done she replied, "I had no right to any kind of personal thoughts, opinions or feelings. Rather I had the duty to obey..."

The Allied alliance

In February 1945, British Prime Minister Winston Churchill, US President Franklin D. Roosevelt, and General Secretary Stalin met in Yalta on the Black Sea. Stalin was at the height of his power having been instrumental in defeating Hitler's forces. Churchill and Roosevelt had been suspicious of the Soviet leader during World War II, but they needed him. The two leaders feared that Stalin had post-war plans for the Red Army to occupy Eastern Europe. Their fears proved correct.

The Yalta agreements promised free elections in the Baltics and Eastern Europe, but the Soviets fixed the elections and communists took power. In Bulgaria, the monarch Boris III had ruled like a dictator. Once the communists took power, the country became the most loyal of the Soviet **satellite states**.

The Allied leaders meet at Yalta in 1945, (from left to right) British Prime Minister Winston Churchill, US President Franklin D. Roosevelt, and General Secretary Joseph Stalin. An unnatural but essential alliance sealed at Yalta ensured the defeat of Nazi Germany. However, as soon as the war was over, the united front collapsed and the Cold War began.

The Cold War

The Cold War between the United States and the USSR began almost immediately after the end of World War II. The change from wartime allies to political enemies happened in less than a year. It was a war on many fronts – political, scientific, and technological – but there was never any military action. The Cold War was a political chess game in which both sides tried to outmanoeuvre the other through economic pressure and spying. Many countries were completely devastated after World War II, but the United States and the USSR matched each other in industrial strength, military might, and resources. They also had the same desire to spread their influence around the world, taking war-devastated nations under their wings in order to strengthen the global influence of their politics, democracy or communism.

Conrad Schumann, an East German border guard, reported for duty on 15 August, 1961. When the other guards had their backs turned, the young soldier made his break to the West to join his family who had fled earlier. He became one of the most famous East German escapees.

THE BERLIN WALL

Built in 1961, the Berlin Wall is arguably the most famous symbol of the Cold War. Dividing Berlin into East and West, the wall drew a physical line between two systems of government, democracy in the West and communism in the East. Cement and barbed wire barriers separated families and friends.

Political and economic conditions meant life was very hard in the East, while people in the West were wealthy and free. Over the years, thousands of people tried to escape to West Berlin by hiding in car boots to cross the border. In 1964, 57 people escaped through a 145-metre- (475-foot-) long tunnel.

Like millions in the Eastern bloc, David is a victim of the Cold War and the closing off of communist countries. The checkpoints and crossing points between East and West Berlin were symbolic of the whole Cold War political divide between the United States and the USSR.

"They" and the thought police

I am David is a novel about mid-20th century persecution. Across the Eastern bloc, individual freedoms, such as speech, movement, and even thought, were restricted in order to keep the population under control and loyal to the communist cause. In his camp, David has trained himself not to think and not to ask questions. After he has escaped, David wishes that he had asked Johannes more questions about the outside world. People in communist countries were controlled and influenced in many ways, and David's ideas about freedom are affected even after he escapes the camp.

The camps, like this one in the town of Vorkuta in the Arctic North, were controlled with watchtowers, electric barbed wire fences, and searchlights. Any prisoner seen escaping would be shot.

In Italy, David meets and stays with the del 'Varchi family. Rather than play with the children, he prefers to spend time in the library reading books, which he has never been able to do before. He wants a book that was published before 1917, the year of the Russian Revolution, "to be sure what was in it was true and not something they had made up". David's idea that everything was good and honest before 1917 may be somewhat biased due to his suffering in the camp. Life under the tsars before the Russian Revolution had not been always truthful and fair, either.

Suppression of the arts

The regimes of Stalin and Hitler persecuted anyone considered a threat to authority. Writers, historians, and free-thinkers were seen as particularly dangerous and were among Stalin and Hitler's first targets. Many fled the USSR and Nazi-occupied countries and wrote in freedom in other countries. The "brain drain" of intellectuals and scientists had long-term consequences for German and Eastern bloc culture and industry.

Stalin and Nikita Khrushchev (who became leader of the USSR after Stalin's death in 1953) with children in Moscow, 1937. Stalin controlled the state press to make him appear to be talking to the people of the Soviet Union all the time. The reality was very different. He only ever directly addressed his people twice.

When Hitler Stole Pink Rabbit by Judith Kerr tells the true story of her father fleeing Nazi Germany the day after Hitler became Chancellor because, as a writer, his name was one of the "first on the list". The rest of the family followed him, becoming refugees like David, travelling first to Switzerland, then to France, and finally finding safety in England.

REWRITING HISTORY

*Stalin had many areas of Russian contemporary and historical life **doctored** to favour his own political intentions. He also imposed his version of events over the Russian arts world. Boris Pasternak was one of Russia's most famous writers. His novel, Dr Zhivago, was banned due to its "un-Bolshevik" portrayal of the Russian Revolution. It details the horrors of October 1917. Although this novel was completed in 1956, it only appeared in print in Moscow in 1988 – nearly thirty years after Pasternak's death.*

Innocent minds

Both Stalin and Hitler realized the importance of educating the young to ensure they were both obedient and devoted to their political causes as adults. Schools in the USSR taught revised Soviet history with school books doctored to present the world according to **Stalinism**. In German schools, Nazi Party members instructed children about the purity of the **Aryan** race. At the del 'Varchi house, David learns from Maria and her brothers that their schools are free to teach the truth. He realizes that, "The children were not told what they were to think. They learnt proper things – about history [...]"

A 1936 Soviet poster portrays Stalin as the "Friend of the little children".

Stalin attempted to influence the next generation through a youth organization called The Pioneers. It was similar to the Scouts movement, but with one key difference – it had a communist attitude. Right across the Eastern bloc, young people joined these groups wearing red neckties, taking part in camps, and absorbing political teachings. Like the later Nazi version, Hitler Youth, The Pioneers were instilled with principles of obedience to Stalinism.

A NEW NATIONAL ANTHEM

By the start of World War II, Stalin's influence over cultural life had reached new levels as the leader himself became the focus of literature, music, paintings, and film. The new Soviet national anthem, written by A. O. Audienko in 1936, reflected this new culture with its lyrics making Stalin god-like.

O great Stalin, O leader of the peoples,
Thou who broughtest man to birth [...]
Thou who makest bloom the spring [...]
Thou, splendour of my spring, O thou,
Sun reflected by millions of hearts.

Country before family

Pavlik Morozov was thirteen years old when he was chosen to be an example to all Soviet children. Pavlik had apparently informed on his own father who had tried to sabotage the collectivization of their village.

Pavlik was murdered by villagers who were angered at this betrayal. His image and story was seen and heard at Pioneer camps across the USSR with leaders using him as an example of **patriotism**.

LOST CHILDHOOD

Stalin and Hitler's regimes robbed millions of children of a secure childhood. David's story is symbolic of children around the world who fall victim to extreme political systems. In 1942, Anne Frank, a thirteen-year-old Jewish girl, and her family were forced into hiding in an Amsterdam attic. Like David, she maintained her belief that "people are truly good at heart" despite all the evil she witnessed. Anne (seen here in 1940) wrote about her experiences in a diary which was published after the war. Today, The Diary of Anne Frank is the most famous personal account of the Nazi persecution of the Jews.

The journey home

David must struggle to regain his childhood. His journey to self-knowledge is a structure found in many stories in all cultures. Within this literary tradition, Holm builds her character's journey into a series of tests where he has to use his new-found faith and knowledge to resist those who persecute him.

David's lowest point is not in the camp, but when he has left the del 'Varchi house after being part of a family for a time. In a prayer to his God, he realizes that freedom and beauty are not enough to live for, "Not when you know there's love and you haven't anyone you belong to." This is the cruellest thing life has shown him yet, either inside or outside the camp.

In the "Testimony of Shmuel Krakowsky" Shmuel, who was imprisoned in Theresienstadt, wrote:

We knew [...] that our liberation was a matter of days or even hours. Unfortunately, for people exhausted after the suffering of the death march and years of starvation, those hours of waiting for the liberators to come seemed very long. Each hour stretched to eternity.

The interior of the main synagogue in the Jewish Quarter of Prague, Czech Republic. The walls record the names of all the Jewish people rounded up and taken to the death camps.

Another important character David meets is the one who holds the key to his identity, Fraulein Bang. Challenges remain for David on his journey, but he is better able to cope because he has real hope and knowledge for the first time.

After liberation, inmates had to remain in the camps until food and medical supplies could be distributed. Many of the liberating soldiers suffered from terrible memories as they struggled to come to terms with the scale of what they found. Here, US soldiers escort liberated prisoners from Konzentrationslager Nackerholtz, France, November 1944.

Precious freedom

In both Nazi and Soviet camps, the hope of freedom kept inmates going through dreadful hardship. David has held on to a vague idea of freedom from Johannes. He fears that waiting for freedom might take "years", and that the waiting "might kill him in the end". In World War II, prisoners in Nazi camps waited in a similar way, day by day, hoping that help would arrive.

PERMANENT SCARS

Confronting the nightmares of their memories and telling people about the horrors of the camps is something many survivors have tried to do. David gradually rids himself of some of the physical influences of the camp: from washing himself, to cutting his hair, to wearing "ordinary" clothes, but he cannot escape from "the terror, the hatred". Eventually he breaks down on the doorstep of his mother's house in Copenhagen.

The Red Scare

Threatening or intimidating political situations can occur anywhere. Attempts to control people's thinking and change attitudes can also happen in democracies. By not specifying where and when David's story takes place, David's experience becomes symbolic of many different systems of oppression that can occur anywhere, and at anytime.

After World War II, there was a real fear that communism would spread beyond the borders of the Soviet Union to the West. In the United States, in particular, this caused grave concern. Many US people saw the communist system as the opposite of their own country's values.

In a reversal of Stalin's persecution of free-thinkers and political opponents, Senator Joseph McCarthy led the persecution of communists in the United States. During the Cold War, the US government was concerned about Soviet spies working at all levels of politics. In 1950, Senator McCarthy began a campaign to rid society and the US government of communists. The fear of communism became extreme in the United States, and anyone speaking out against McCarthy and his methods was suspected of being a "Red".

Many US citizens supported McCarthy's investigation. In the 1950s, the "Red Scare" touched on popular political concerns that the "red under the bed" threatened US values and ways of life.

Blacklisting

Just being accused of supporting communism was enough to guarantee personal or professional ruin. In a naming and shaming process, known as blacklisting, McCarthy accused hundreds of people of supporting communism – from famous actors in Hollywood to everyday middle-class people.

Arthur Miller wrote about his experiences of the anti-communist witch-hunts in the 1950s, and how they informed his writing in the *The Crucible in History and Other Essays*, 2000:

> *It would probably never have occurred to me to write a play about the Salem witch trials of 1692 had I not seen some astonishing correspondences with that calamity in the America of the late 40s and early 50s. My basic need was to respond to a phenomenon which, with only small exaggeration, one could say paralyzed a whole generation and in a short time dried up the habits of trust and toleration in public discourse.*

At the same time, membership of the American Communist Party (ACP) was growing. The US government rounded up ACP members and anyone suspected of being sympathetic to communism. McCarthy investigated all suspects. The term McCarthyism has come to mean any government activity that seeks to suppress unfavourable political or social views, while often suspending or ignoring civil rights.

Anti-communist witch-hunts

McCarthy's accusations were often based on unreliable evidence. The comic actor Charlie Chaplin and playwright Arthur Miller were both questioned by the Senator. Refusing to name people he thought were sympathetic to communism, Miller was found guilty of contempt of Congress in 1957, but his conviction was **quashed** the following year. Chaplin's political sympathies always lay with the workers. Several of his films, notably *Modern Times*, depict the dismal situation of workers and the poor. Accused by McCarthy of "un-American activities", Chaplin left the United States in 1952 and lived in Switzerland for the rest of his life.

A scene from a 1955 production of Arthur Miller's play, *The Crucible*. Miller used the Salem witch trials of 1692 as a **metaphor** for the McCarthy witch-hunts of the 1950s. Miller wanted to show that this style of persecution could occur at any time and any place.

Propaganda and controlling information

From the time of the Egyptian pharaohs, powerful figures in many cultures have tried to create an exaggerated positive image of themselves. In order to remain firmly in power, leaders such as Stalin and Hitler felt they had to make their presence felt in all areas of life from statues and huge civic portraits, to school books and the face on a stamp. They wanted to create an image of themselves as the defender, friend, and father of the people. Through fear and authority "they" became larger than life.

БУДЕМ ДОСТОЙНЫМИ СЫНАМИ И ДОЧЕРЬМИ
НАШЕЙ ВЕЛИКОЙ ПАРТИИ ЛЕНИНА-СТАЛИНА

Image control was everything in Stalin's regime. The ministry for internal affairs, which housed Stalin's propaganda office, created a feeling that the leader was always watching and looking over the population. The caption on this poster says: "Let us be worthy sons and daughters of our great party of Lenin and Stalin."

State press

In 1930s Russia there was only one nationally available newspaper, which was called *Pravda* (also *Izvestia*). Ironically meaning "Truth", the paper was a central part of Stalin's **propaganda** campaign to win public support. Since there was no television, controlling the press meant that Stalin's "truths" could be repeated many times over. David sees any tampering with the truth as dangerous.

The Main Administration for Literary and Publishing Affairs, *Glavlit*, was created in 1922. It was responsible for **censorship**. All books were carefully checked for anti-revolutionary comments or criticisms so that only the official version of events got published. Paper was withheld from writers suspected of being anti-Stalin. One of the first luxuries David buys himself is a notepad – something he has never had – so that he can practice his writing. In 1932, the Union of Writers was created to produce literature promoting the communist cause.

Stalin used *Pravda* in his national propaganda campaign.

THE SECRET SPEECH

*In 1956, after Stalin's death, the new Soviet leader Nikita Khrushchev gave a speech to a closed session of the Communist Party. Repeatedly **denouncing** Stalin, Khrushchev said that Stalin's regime had been "monstrous". Khrushchev started a process of reversing or neutralizing the influence of Stalin by changing his **policies**, removing monuments dedicated to him, and renaming places named in his honour.*

After the 1917 Revolution, a large number of Russian cities were renamed to make them sound more revolutionary and communist. This culture of changing the names of places was widespread. In 1914, Russia and Germany were at war. The city of St Petersburg was renamed Petrograd because the original name sounded too German. In 1924, Petrograd became Leningrad in honour of Lenin, and in 1991, with the fall of communism, the city became St Petersburg once again.

Powerful influences

In the labour camps of the Eastern bloc special papers were printed with "news". These propaganda papers were written to inform prisoners what they were doing for the country's progress. Newspapers with names such as *Perekovka* (Reshaping) were printed and circulated. They were designed to change prisoners' minds and turn them into dedicated builders of communism. In his camp, David does not know anything of the outside world other than what Johannes or the guard tell him for his own protection. Johannes teaches David to protect himself from being manipulated, telling him, "If you never allow other people to influence what you're really like, then you've something no one can take from you." Outside of the camps, Soviet propaganda made the Five Year Plans very popular with young people who believed they were helping to create a better world through communism.

FILM PROPAGANDA

With the arrival of cinema, Stalin ordered propaganda films to be made about labour camps, such as Solovetsky, to promote the policy of re-education through hard work. Film directors also responded positively to the Revolution. Made in 1925, The Battleship Potemkin (a scene of which is shown below) is a silent film that glorifies the real-life failed uprising of a battleship crew in 1905. Sergei Eisenstein deliberately directed the film as propaganda and edited it in a way that would make the audience feel sympathy for the rebellious sailors of the battleship, and hatred for the officers.

Propaganda is a tool of oppressive regimes around the world. In Iraq, Saddam Hussein's **personality cult** affected the entire society. He had thousands of portraits, posters, and statues put up in his honour. Upon Saddam's capture in 2003, ordinary Iraqis immediately attacked these symbols of his oppressive regime. Giant statues were knocked down by cranes (above), and remnants of Saddam's personality cult were destroyed.

Strategic conflict

Soviet propaganda was not only used inside the USSR. In fact, an "iron curtain" of political secrecy existed even before World War II. Outside media was either banned from broadcasting within the Soviet Union, or suffered censorship. Western readers had little direct access to information from within the USSR.

Anne Holm writes about the failings of a system that does not allow truth or human freedoms, and uses David as a channel through which the reader

(and characters such as Maria) can learn some truths about the terrible persecution that occurred.

The Soviet government boasted of its achievements to Western Europe and the United States, but it never allowed experts or scientists from outside the country to check on the accuracy of the claims. However, the Soviets made many genuine scientific advances during the Cold War, particularly in space technology and weapons development.

A SEARCH FOR TRUTH

Nearly fifty years after he had been liberated from Auschwitz, Primo Levi wrote the following on the privilege of knowing the whole truth:

"The world in which we westerners live has some grave faults and dangers, but when compared to the countries in which democracy is smothered [. . .] our world has a tremendous advantage: everyone can know everything about everything."

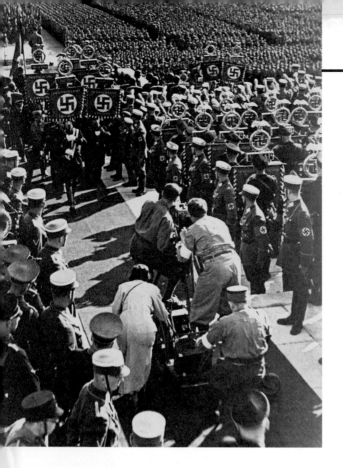

Both Hitler and Stalin used the medium of film for propaganda purposes. Perhaps the best-known example of film propaganda is *Triumph of the Will*, directed by the German film-maker Leni Riefenstahl (seen here crouching next to the camera). The film documents the 1934 Nazi Party Congress in Nuremberg. Hitler praised the film as being "an incomparable glorification of the power and beauty of our Movement."

The power of words

In their own countries, Hitler and Mussolini also used a variety of propaganda tactics to gain support and to limit opposition. Both leaders were gifted speakers and thrived on addressing mass rallies where they could exploit **mob mentality** and patriotic pride.

State manipulation

Germany's mass media was under the control of his propaganda chief, Goebbels. He persuaded many Germans that Hitler would save them from the economic hardship Germany experienced after World War I. People thought the Nazi Party would again make Germany a strong and wealthy country. Mussolini also created a **fascist** state through the use of terror and propaganda. Using his charisma, total control of the media, and intimidation of political rivals he disassembled the existing democratic government system and wiped out all obvious opposition.

In Germany, Hitler appointed a personal film-maker to make countless propaganda films for the German Nazi Party, while in Italy Mussolini spent much of his time on propaganda. A trained journalist himself, he carefully supervised printed and visual media to create the illusion that **fascism** was the great political movement of the century, replacing democracy.

BIG BROTHER IS WATCHING

*Written in 1948, George Orwell's novel Nineteen Eighty-Four is a dark, **dystopian** tale set in a country where speech is doctored and the Thought Police are in control. The novel is about the dangers of a **totalitarian** society. Ruled by Big Brother, the land of Oceania is symbolic of any system of government where civil freedoms are limited, such as Hitler's Germany or Stalin's Soviet Union. In Oceania, "they" are everywhere.*

Yevgeny Zamyatin was a Russian author, most famous for his novel We, first published in English in 1924. It is the story of a nightmarish future, which influenced George Orwell's Nineteen Eighty-Four. Zamyatin supported the Revolution, but opposed the censorship of the Bolshevik regime. His works were increasingly critical of Bolshevism, which led to them being banned.

Arthur Koestler was a journalist, novelist, and political campaigner. His most famous work is Darkness at Noon, published in 1940. It is a novel about a Communist Party official who falls victim to Stalin's purges. Koestler believed in the progress that communism was supposed to bring, but became disillusioned by the way it was being carried out in the USSR.

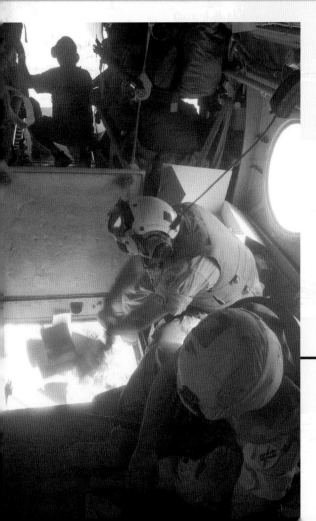

Propaganda

During World War II, Soviet and Allied Forces used propaganda to demoralize and destabilize Nazi forces and the German population. Pamphlets containing insulting information about Hitler and showing the Allies advancing to victory were dropped from airplanes. During the war in Afghanistan in 2002, US and British forces dropped leaflets explaining what was happening, and why, in an attempt to win over the support of the local people.

Pamphlets were also dropped from US airplanes during the Iraq war of 2003.

A story for all time

Anne Holm wrote other books after *I am David*, but none repeated this story's international impact and lasting appeal. David's story celebrates freedom and the power of hope through a dark episode in world history. After a difficult journey David finds happiness and defeats the system that imprisoned him. Holm described herself as politically "conservative". But her novel clearly rejects political systems that lack freedom of thought and expression, whether they are communist or fascist.

I am David may not itself have affected world history, but it did show that adult themes could be presented to younger readers with a startling and lasting effect. The novel was part of an expanding group of political books that were being read by young adults, including *Animal Farm* by George Orwell, based on the Russian Revolution, and *The Silver Sword* by Ian Seraillier, which is based on true stories of Polish refugee children.

The Berlin Wall was finally knocked down in November 1989. East and West Berlin were once again united.

At the time Anne Holm was writing *I am David*, various alarming events were happening elsewhere in the world. The Berlin Wall was built and, in 1962, the **Cuban Missile Crisis** brought the world to the brink of nuclear war. The world was changing again as the balance of power rocked awkwardly between East and West. Anne Holm wrote her novel in the early 1960s, over fifteen years after the last Nazi camp was liberated and after the Eastern bloc countries became closed societies. The events of World War II were still fresh and inspired writers to tell individual tales of survival, courage, and hope.

The beginnings of protest

After Stalin's death in 1953, the Soviet hold on the Eastern bloc gradually weakened as more people demanded democracy. By the time Holm was writing *I am David*, the anti-communist Hungarian revolution of 1956 had already happened. Eventually quashed, it was however a sign that people power could try to overturn decades of oppressive rule.

ANYTIME, ANYWHERE

Today there are still countries, such as North Korea and China, run by communist governments. In these countries it is still dangerous to speak out against the ruling powers. In 1989, 100,000 people gathered in Tiananmen Square, Beijing, to protest against the communist government. In response, the Chinese authorities sent tanks and troops to confront the demonstrators and many protestors were killed. Even today, the Chinese government dismisses any suggested death figures. The international community condemned the actions of the Chinese government and has since put pressure on China to improve its human rights record.

A classic image of resisting oppression; a single Chinese student obstructs a line of Chinese Government tanks heading towards Tiananmen Square, 1989. This image has become a powerful symbol of individuals standing up to dictatorships and seeking positive political change all over the world.

Many of the death and labour camps in Germany, Poland, and the former Eastern bloc are now social history museums. Education is vital if the horrors of persecution are not to be forgotten.

A tide of change

By the 1980s, political relations had improved between the United States and the USSR. Agreements to abolish some types of nuclear weapons were reached and the Soviet leader, Mikhail Gorbachev, encouraged democratic elections across the Eastern bloc. This period was called glasnost (being public, or open). The last effects of Stalin's rule were finally being overcome. Many of the labour camps were closed down, and thousands of political prisoners like David were freed.

From 1989 onwards, many governments in Eastern Europe were overthrown by the will of people wanting to live and think freely.

Just like David, these people had learnt to "think again without being afraid" and they seized the chance to change history. Jubilant West and East Germans danced together on top of the Berlin Wall, and Czechs gathered in Wenceslas Square, Prague, to hail a new era. Even in Bulgaria the demand for change was too strong to resist and, in 1990, the first free elections for nearly sixty years were held there. The Cold War was over, and the "iron curtain" that Churchill had seen descending over the continent had been lifted at last.

The director of the 2003 film version of *I am David*, Paul Feig, said,

> **We all have a tendency to take the freedoms that we experience in our daily lives for granted, since few of us have ever been exposed to true injustice and persecution. [...] sometimes you have to risk a lot in order to attain freedom.**

Through David's story, Anne Holm shows the importance of freedom and the value of hope.

Cover story

Many different editions of *I am David* have been published with a range of meaningful cover images. The choice of image for a book's front cover often reflects the politics of the day, the culture of the country the book is published in, and the choices of the publisher. Most Western publications of the book produce a cover showing a boy walking alone through a bleak landscape that offers him nothing. His face is often unseen as if he has no identity, and perhaps to show he is one among millions. In other editions, David's eyes stare out from behind barbed wire showing a face that cannot be shocked or react to pain anymore.

Photographs, such as this, which show a boy walking through a bleak landscape, or on a journey, have been used for the cover of *I am David*.

David in the 21st century

After the end of the Cold War, Anne Holm's novel continues to be relevant today. David's epic journey, along with his struggle to stay free and to find out who he is, appeals to modern readers and film-makers just as it did when it was first published. As he stands on the doorstep of his mother's house in Copenhagen, David finally realizes the truth of Fraulein Bang's words, "All suffering has an end [. . .] if only you wait long enough."

David eventually finds his way to a home, but others are not so lucky. The 21st century already has examples of displaced people seeking a home. Today, in many parts of the world, there are other Davids; refugees who travel across countries and continents fleeing persecution in the hope of finding a home.

On 14 December, 1950, the Office of the United Nations High Commissioner for Refugees was established by the United Nations General Assembly. The agency leads and co-ordinates international action to protect refugees and to resolve refugee problems worldwide. Its primary purpose is to safeguard the rights and well-being of refugees so they can seek **asylum** and find safe refuge in another state or country. Today, more than 6,000 staff in more than 116 countries help around 19 million people.

The official logo for the United Nations High Commission for Refugees, which has helped an estimated 50 million people restart their lives since it was founded over fifty years ago.

Thousands of refugees fleeing civil war in Sudan wait for transportation to refugee camps in neighbouring Chad. In many parts of the world people are still victimized on the grounds of their faith, colour, tribe, or thinking. In some places, the mass displacement of people needs international assistance to prevent human disasters.

LETTERS FOR FREEDOM

Amnesty International is a worldwide movement of people who campaign for internationally recognized human rights. With the "Universal Declaration of Human Rights" at its core of values, Amnesty members write to governments all over the world to demand action on behalf of political prisoners or torture victims.

I am David – the legacy

Anne Holm's stirring human story about a child's unbreakable spirit in the face of huge obstacles still affects people today, over forty years since it was written. The book's powerful vision of the world through the eyes of a child is timeless. As David journeys across spectacular landscapes and foreign cultures, he encounters sights, sounds, friendships, and emotions that are exciting and completely new to him. David's camp experience and story is symbolic of countless others. His long march to freedom has echoes throughout history and leaves the reader with an understanding of what it is to be hunted, and yet to have hope.

RETURN TO TERROR?

In recent years, Stalin's cult of personality has re-emerged in the former Soviet Union. Fed up with economic instability, a recent poll showed that over 25 percent of Russians would vote for him if he were alive. For Holm's David, however, Stalin's system represents everything that is cruel, treacherous, and dishonest. Outside of the camp he has learnt how precious freedom and truth are.

TIMELINE

1848	Marx and Engels publish *The Communist Manifesto*.
1914	World War I begins.
1917	Russian Revolution begins.
1918	Russian civil war begins and lasts for three years.
1918	Tsar Nicholas II and his family are executed.
1918	Germany is defeated, World War I is over.
1922	Anne Holm is born on 10 September.
1922	Literary censorship begins in the USSR.
1924	Death of Lenin. Stalin becomes leader of USSR.
1925	Mussolini's Press Laws dictate that all journalists must be registered fascists.
1925	Pro-communist, pro-revolution film *The Battleship Potemkin* is made.
1928	Mussolini becomes dictator of Italy.
1928	The first Five Year Plan begins.
1930s	Closure of places of worship in the USSR.
1932	Soviet Union of Writers is created to write communist literature.
1933	Hitler is appointed Chancellor of Germany.
1936	The start of Stalin's Great Purge.
1936	Germany forms alliances with Italy and Japan.
1939	World War II begins. USSR and Germany invade Poland.
1939	Red Army invades Finland.
1940	German troops invade Denmark. Auschwitz concentration camp is built.
1941	Japan attacks US Pacific Fleet in Pearl Harbor, Hawaii. United States declares war on Japan.
1941	Hitler invades Russia in Operation Barbarossa.
1942	Nazi Final Solution begins.
1942	Battle of Stalingrad begins.
1943	Danish Jews are evacuated to Sweden.
1945	Soviet Army liberates Auschwitz.
1945	George Orwell's *Animal Farm* is published.

KEY	
	World history
	Local/national history (Russia/ Soviet Union)
	Author's life
	I Am David

1945	United Nations is created. Germany surrenders, May. Denmark is liberated, and her monarch returns. Japan surrenders after atomic bombs are dropped on Hiroshima and Nagasaki, August. World War II ends. Start of the Cold War.
1946	Churchill makes "iron curtain" speech.
1948	Universal Declaration of Human Rights is drafted. George Orwell's *Nineteen Eighty-Four* is published.
1949	Anne Holm marries Johan Christian Holm, a coin and medal expert.
1949	North Atlantic Treaty Organization (NATO) is formed.
1950	Senator McCarthy begins anti-communist inquiries in United States.
1951	United Nations High Commission for Refugees is established.
1953	Death of Stalin.
1953	Arthur Miller's play *The Crucible* is performed for the first time.
1955	The Warsaw Pact is signed uniting USSR and Eastern European communist countries.
1956	Khrushchev denounces Stalin in the Secret Speech. Hungarian Revolution.
1961	Construction of Berlin Wall.
1962	*One Day in the Life of Ivan Denizovich* by Aleksandr Solzhenitsyn is published.
1962	Cuban Missile Crisis, October.
1963	Danish publication of *David*. The novel wins the Prize for Best Scandinavian Children's Book.
1965	First English language edition of *I am David* is published. The novel is awarded the ALA Notable Book award and Boys Club of America Junior book Award.
1973	*The Gulag Archipelago* by Aleksandr Solzhenitsyn is published.
1989	Soviet-bloc countries relax travel restrictions.
1989	Berlin Wall falls. Chinese students protest in Tiananmen Square, China.
1991	Collapse of the Soviet Union.
1998	Anne Holm dies.
2003	Film version of *I am David* is released.

FURTHER INFORMATION

The edition of *I am David* used in the writing of this book was published by Egmont in 2000.

Further reading

Books about Stalin's Russia and the Gulag

Orwell, George. *Animal Farm*. (Secker and Warburg, 1945)

Orwell, George. *Nineteen Eighty-Four*. (Secker and Warburg, 1949)

Shalamov, Varlam. *Kolyma Tales*. (W. W. Norton, 1980)

Solzhenitsyn, Aleksandr. *One Day in the Life of Ivan Denisovich*. (Farrar, Straus, and Giroux, 1962)

Solzhenitsyn, Aleksandr. *The Gulag Archipelago 1918–1956*. (Collins, 1973)

Books about Hitler's Germany and the Holocaust

Frank, Anne (ed. Otto Frank/trans. Susan Massotty). *The Diary of Anne Frank*. (Doubleday, 1952)

Kerr, Judith. *When Hitler Stole Pink Rabbit*. (Collins, 2002)

Levi, Primo (trans. Stuart Woolf). *If This is A Man/The Truce*. (Simon & Schuster, 1996)

Schneider, Helga. *Let Me Go*. (Vintage, 2005)

Serraillier, Ian. *The Silver Sword*. (Abelard Schuman, 1959)

Books about life in communist China/Other

Adeline Mah, Yen. *Falling Leaves*. (Longman, 2001)

Ballard, J. G. *Empire of the Sun*. (Gollancz, 1984)

Chang, Jung. *Wild Swans: Three Daughters of China*. (HarperPerennial, 2004)

Xinran. *The Good Women of China: Hidden Voices*. (Vintage, 2006)

Useful websites

Stalin and the Soviet Union

www.osa.ceu.hu/gulag/ – Open Society Archives on the Gulag forced labour camps.

www.spartacus.schoolnet.co.uk – useful resource on Stalin and his leadership.

Nazi Germany and the Final Solution

www.bbc.co.uk/history – for various articles about World War II and Hitler.

www.yadvashem.org – Yad Vashem, The Holocaust Martyrs' and Heroes' Remembrance Authority.

www.wiesenthal.com – Simon Wiesenthal Center.

www.deathcamps.info – comprehensive information on the Nazi death camps.

Movies

Empire of the Sun (1987). Adapted from the novel of the same name by J. G. Ballard, directed by Steven Spielberg, and starring Christian Bale. A young English boy struggles to survive under Japanese occupation during World War II.

Life is Beautiful (1997). Directed by Roberto Benigni.

Schindler's List (1993). Adapted from the novel *Schindler's Ark* by Thomas Kenneally, directed by Steven Spielberg, and starring Liam Neeson.

Stalin: Inside the Terror (2003). Directed by Tony Bulley, this is a documentary based around revealing interviews with family members.

Places to visit

Imperial War Musuem, London – www.iwm.org.uk

The Anne Frank House, Amsterdam, The Netherlands – www.annefrank.org

United States Holocaust Memorial Museum – www.ushmm.org

Many of the former camps are open as museums. Auschwitz-Birkenau in Poland, Matthausen in Austria, and Terezin in the Czech Republic are all open to visitors.

GLOSSARY

allegiance loyalty

ally friend in agreement

aristocracy the nobility

Aryan person of non-Jewish descent, regarded by the Nazis as racially superior

asylum protection from danger in a neutral place

bloc united group of countries with a shared aim

Bolshevik supporter of Lenin's revolution/party

bourgeoisie middle class, or wealthy

capitalist supporter of capitalism, economic and political system in which a country's trade and industry are controlled by private owners for profit, rather than by the state

censorship banning or deleting content considered to be politically dangerous

Cold War hostile, but non-violent, relations between the United States and the Soviet Union

collectivization running or organizing a large group of farms together, with people sharing labour and tools

commandant officer in charge

communism belief in a classless society that shares the state's wealth and gives ownership of all property to the state

communist supporter of communism

concentration camp prison camp

conscript enlist compulsorily into the armed forces

corrupt willing to act dishonestly in return for money or personal gain

Cuban Missile Crisis extremely tense confrontation between the United States and the Soviet Union over the Soviet deployment of nuclear missiles in Cuba, October 1962. It is regarded as being the closest the Cold War came to nuclear war.

death camp Nazi-run camps where Jews and other minorities were murdered on a large scale

democracy system of government based on the principle of majority decision-making and elected representatives

denounce criticize or condemn somebody

deported to be banished from one's own country

depose remove from office

dictator leader who rules with absolute power, usually by force, leading to a dictatorship

discourse written or spoken communication or debate

doctored altered, changed, manipulated

dystopian imaginary place or society in which everything is bad

egalitarian belief that all people are equal and deserve equal rights

ethnic group sharing cultural characteristics

exile force somebody against their will to leave their country

exploit take advantage of

fascism system of government with a dictator, repression of all opposition, and extreme pride in one's country

fascist supporter of fascism

Five Year Plans Stalin's plans for rapid economic development

genocide murder of an entire ethnic or religious group

Gulag political prison or camp in the former Soviet Union

illiterate unable to read

labour camp prison where prisoners are forced to do hard physical work

malnourished lack of proper nutrition

manifesto written declaration of principles, usually by a political group

metaphor figure of speech used to symbolize something to which it is not literally applicable

mob mentality losing individual judgement and getting caught up in the crowd

monarchy royal family

Nazi member of the National Socialist German Worker's Party

neutral not supporting either side in a conflict or dispute

newsreels films of the news that people watched in cinemas before television was invented

North Atlantic Treaty Organization (NATO) international organization for collective security established in 1949, in support of the North Atlantic Treaty signed in Washington, DC, on 4 April 1949

occupied country that has been taken over by an invading force

patriotism being proud of one's country

persecution treating people cruelly or unfairly because of their ethnic origin or religious beliefs

personality cult political system of devotion in which a country's ruler encourages praise of himself and his deeds to the point of affecting every aspect of society

policies programmes of actions

prison camp camp where prisoners of war are kept

prisoner of war (POW) someone who has been captured and imprisoned by the enemy in a war

propaganda publicity used to promote a particular idea or policy

purge get rid of opponents

quashed stopped

regime form of oppressive government

resistance secret groups fighting political or military occupation

revolution overthrow of a government in favour of a new system

satellite states smaller countries which are both dependent upon and influenced by a larger, more powerful country

satire use of humour to expose or criticize people's vices or stupidity

serfdom enslaved system of labour in 19th century-Russia

socialist somebody who believes in socialism/communism and an equal society

Soviet Union (USSR) Union of Soviet Socialist Republics, a union of workers councils from Central and Eastern Europe joined to make a powerful nation state. The USSR disbanded in 1991.

Stalinism ideology and policies adopted by Joseph Stalin, based on centralization, totalitarianism, and communism

superpower hugely powerful country with a great deal of influence, like the Soviet Union during the Cold War

totalitarian dictatorial: a government in which a single party without opposition rules over all aspects of life

tsar Russian emperor

tyranny cruel or oppressive government or rule

U-boats German submarines

United Nations organization of nations that was formed in 1945 to promote peace, security, and international co-operation

violation act of breaking a rule

Warsaw Pact military organization of Central and Eastern European Communist states established in 1955 to counter the perceived threat from the NATO alliance. The Pact was officially dissolved in July 1991.

INDEX